Their Backs
to the Sea

Ahu Tongariki, as seen from the sea.

Their Backs to the Sea

Poems and photographs

by

Margaret Randall

WingsPress

San Antonio, Texas
2009

Their Backs to the Sea © 2009 by Margaret Randall
Cover art: "Tongariki Through Rano Raraku" © 2009 by Jane Norling

First Edition

ISBN-13: 978-0-916727-61-1

Wings Press
627 E. Guenther
San Antonio, Texas 78210
Phone/fax: (210) 271-7805

On-line catalogue and ordering:
www.wingspress.com
All Wings Press titles are distributed to the trade by
Independent Publishers Group
www.ipgbook.com

Library of Congress Cataloging-in-Publication Data:

Randall, Margaret, 1936-
  Their backs to the sea : poems and photographs / by Margaret
Randall. -- 1st ed.
      p. cm.
  ISBN 978-0-916727-61-1 (pbk. : alk. paper)
  I. Title.
  PS3535.A56277T47 2009
  811'.52--dc22
                            2009020702

For Barbara and Jane, co-adventurers

Photographs are indicated by italics.
All photographs were taken by Margaret Randall.

Contents

Pulling the Island Behind

Easter Island, Rapa Nui, or simply the land
your ancestors felt no need to name,
place that receives me now
eager and awkward: my eyes
hauling picture-book images,
mouth filled with questions
juggling answers as I breathe.

I will think of you as an island
without color on a map,
your first people dizzied in harmony,
clothed by the land itself:
no reason to signify
that which receives and gives,
asks nothing in return.

Hare Paenga Foundation
Overleaf: Land and seascape

Island Without a Name

The universe is built like an enormous feedback loop,
a loop in which we contribute to the ongoing creation
of not just the present and the future but the past as well.

– John Wheeler*

Lone Pukau

* As quoted in Tim Folger's "Does the Universe Exist if We're Not Looking?"
Discover, June 2000, pp. 44-45.

1

Your tongue swells, its smallest gland
still secretes saliva, lining your mouth
with precious wetness.
Lifetime of days brave oppositional winds,
waves overpowering dual hulls
bound together in defiance
of currents, rain and scorching sun.

Southern Cross imprinted upon
unflinching sky.
Searching eyes follow sun's arc
and lunar calendar traces your course
across, against, and down wind
toward destination
or surprise.

Sea turtle swims, raising her small head
above the rolling surf.
Later you will peck her image in rock
framed by a ring of smaller stones.
She will be cicerone and teacher,
nourish hunger
and the patience of song.

Without compass or other nautical device
dolphins and circling land birds
guided your earliest settlers in.
You say Hotu Matu'a was the first
landing at Anakena with his wife, six sons
and extended family, origin of your lineage
in the stories you remember.

Unyielding Pacific, 1,300 miles west of Chile,
1,260 southeast of Pitcairn,
at 27 point 9 south and 109 point 26 west
in the measurements we use today,
a journey of stars beckoned you then,
exhausted but ready,
to this speck of land.

II

Why did you leave the pungent bounty
of Marquesas, Mangareva, Pitcairn
or Henderson
for this hard triangle
lost in the lonely waters of south central Pacific,
its coast repelling every landing
but one, almost every stretch

of rocky shore menacing, threatening
rather than welcoming
your arrival? Relentless
you struggled ashore, opened your eyes
on this slip of lava: ash and obsidian
anchored by three volcanoes
promising balm to your thirst.

When did you come? Some say 1,200 AD,
others earlier, surely before 800
of our era—an era
that would invade you centuries later
in the crazed imposition of men
bearing crosses, determined to break
your hearts and minds: suffocation of conquest.

III

Sixteen million palms once stood upon this mound
of rocky soil. Rope from the bark
of *hau hau* trees and others whose wood
was good for sea-going craft.
Forest, but only a single intermittent stream,
no river to relieve your thirst: cane juice
rotting your teeth as it kept you alive.

Offshore, bubbling up from saltwater depths
and dangerous rock
a freshwater spring still caresses cracked tongues.
The marshy lakes in the craters
of *Rano Kau, Rano Aroi* and *Rano Raraku*
comfort parched cells,
nourish you still.

Weather was always here: winds attacking
from every direction: above, below,
east, south, west, north. Until the palms
were gone, leaving only their memory.
No more canoes. Twisted paper mulberry
offering only beaten cloth
and mirror-image carvings.

Tides and fevers brought on the nausea
of vertigo: whipping your bodies,
pulling you
from the pleated crests
of ridges squeezed in giant fists,
released when tsunamis sucked
the hissing sea from shore.

IV

Little grew in that shallow soil: sweet potatoes,
yams, taro, guava, sugar, and plantains
in lava-tube caves.
Chicken and vegetables. Fish and seabirds.
Sailing vessels brought Polynesian, then Norwegian rats:
—the shameful delicacy. And much later
sheep: tens of thousands, but not for you.

As if leeching life from rock was not enough
to set family upon family, call forth
survival wars, a taste for human flesh
and successive battles, other arrivals
brought animals not for your sustenance,
languages not for your lips, new rules
that pinned you to careening history.

AhuTongariki, closeup of two Moai

Palm leaf

Banana leaf

V

In 1722 a Dutch admiral may have been the first
to spot your presence, gaze in astonishment
at the guardians standing sentinel
along your shores. His logbook said Easter
and he bestowed the Christian name.
You say *Te Pito o te Henua:* navel
of the world. Rapa Nui.

Later English, French, Germans, Russians,
Chileans, and North Americans
found you, stayed hours or days
before giving up on your loneliness,
carried news of those statues,
their backs to the sea their stoic faces
watching over fields and boat-shaped homes.

In 1862 Peruvian slavers kidnapped 1,500
of your healthiest men
and when protest forced them to return
a single starving boatload, the dozen survivors
brought smallpox and tuberculosis,
reducing your population
to a struggling hundred and ten.

Lay brother Eugene Eyraud stayed years
dogged in his sacrifice, obsessive
to convert, to remake you
in the image of his suffering.
He died content he'd saved every island soul
while you made the sign of the cross
and hid your gods for all to see.

VI

Thus the vast sheep station with 70,000 head.
Thus their fences and your taking:
tradition of dreaming what was needed,
announcing you were coming to get it
and making good on your promise,
but always leaving enough
so your oppressors would not starve.

Assaulting your island again and yet again,
pushing you into a crowded corner:
La compañía explotadora de la Isla de Pascua
—company to exploit the island—
with its history of debt enslavement,
rules imposed by those whose god
still signals plunder and abuse.

Memory stretched by long-range voyaging
you lost the wood for your canoes,
lost the traditional skills
for those explorations of blood
and spirit, but still greeted
the whalers and schooners and steamers
that would change your destiny.

VII

Despite repression, hardship, hunger
and disease,
you gave birth and flourished,
new life opening against the odds.
Neither ravages of foreign invasion
nor cousin blood
could erase you from this place.

Those who arrived and looked and fled,
invented stories for the world:
reverse migrations to fit poor theory:
Inca travelers, aliens from outer space,
Lemuria's lost continent
or a Third Race of Giants
appearing, disappearing, then rising again.

Later some came with open-ended questions:
Mrs. Routledge on her *Mana*, Métraux, Mulloy,
even Heyerdahl who worked so hard
to prove his forced hypothesis.
What was proven possible did not happen,
and as discovery turns
so turn the disappearing pages
of an ancient book

what emerges is this: we cannot unravel
your lost world
without having lived its life, faced the wind
and knelt to chip away
at volcanic tuff turning mountains to men

then moving the magical tonnage miles
to stand in silence, backs to the sea.

We must suffer like you, need like you,
lose what you lost
and hold what you held.
Think like you, bargain
the same solutions to the same problems.
In our lives' safe otherness
there is no imagining yours.

VIII

Questions bulk against the windswept slopes
of grassy hills and dark cliffs.
How did you nourish yourself
with scant rain, thin soil, no coral reef
and few fish, how reconcile yourself
to no more wood, no escape
from 63 square miles lost in the desolate Pacific.

You answer with closed fists
hidden behind your backs,
steadfast gaze focused on goals
that evoke descriptions
such as *childlike* or *trickster,*
as you who remember those who remember
stutter and die.

Isolation and contact: adversarial extremes
of an ongoing argument,
what you made and used
thousands of miles from easier lands
and what you brought with you
when you came, pushing adaptation
one generation to the next.

IX

The *moai:* 288 laying where—thrown
from their *ahu:* stone bases
that served as drying platforms for the dead
then tombs for their bones—they follow
stone's cycle into earth. Almost 400
still stand in the quarry
at *Rano Raraku,* or on its outer flank

amidst picks and hammers, cutting and shaping tools:
implements of an art that stopped one day
as if the artists suddenly departed
those great cavities of negative space,
length of a body here, dismembered head
beyond. I scramble across a nose
discovering it is a nose.

Two hundred and two remain in transit,
their unfinished journey through wind
and light. Eight hundred eighty seven
in all: emerging
through stone birthing canals,
kneeling, walking, standing tall
or gone to recovering earth.

Their eyes—sockets pulling us into vacancy—
are silent now beneath broad overhang
of brow. Some once held eyeballs:
coral, obsidian, red scoria
inserted and then removed,
unleashing or retrieving
mana for those who believed.

Too many outsiders took the sacred relics,
leaving nothing but trinkets
and disease.
Those who learned the language
received some stories
but most discarded your people's memory
in favor of their own.

X

Kohau rongorongo's talking wood
left us rows of tiny characters,
shark-bone incisions on small boards:
a script not yet deciphered
by your descendants
though some recite clan boundaries
or broken genealogies.

Notes meant to invoke memory
and ideas that are key,
not letter for letter, word for word.
Those who insist on looking
for the clues that brought
other ancient scripts to life
still wander beyond the circle.

Now ceremony, now a game: *kai kai*
hands a pattern of crossed string
from one set of fingers to another,
a three-dimensional language
unnoticed by early explorers,
better grasped by those
who neither hear nor speak.

What challenged European ears remained
outside the mirror, flew in the face
of that which God-fearing men
believed could be.
What resisted imagination
remained impossible, unthinkable,
unknown.

Spoken language without a word for virgin,
absence of shame on a woman's shoulders,
colors of rock, grass, wind
erasing the hard rules
imposed by Church and State
when they tried to silence birds
or cancel a table set for three.

Fallen Moai at Ahu Akahanga

Moai fallen face down

XI

At the height of community, 20,000
may have lived and labored
on your accidental land.
Three hundred years carving and hauling
images that held a culture together,
makers and movers
trading art for extra food.

Statues others call similar
I see unique in every gesture:
height, girth, tilt of chin,
presence or depth of eyes,
angle of nose, expression on lips.
Beings as different from one another
as the ancestors they honor.

So who threw the massive figures down
and why?
Again the stories rise and fall,
memory and science
gnawing at lichen-covered rock.
Clan against clan? Artisans rebelling
against those who commissioned their work?

XII

At Orongo the winds blow fierce enough
to sweep me from *Rano Kau's* lip
to the black rocks spitting spray
1,000 feet below. Along the narrow
strip of land between crater and sea
grass covers the Birdman houses
waiting in bermed repose.

Motu Kao Kao's guano-spattered pinnacle
rises from foam-tipped waves
and a fishing boat with five or six men
is a toy as it rocks and bobs
off its starboard side.
Power and defeat still echo
from these heights to the scene of the crime.

Makemake holds court on rock face weathered
by years, wind, rain and a chant
still heard in hearts that call
across pulled overlay of time. *Manu tara,*
sooty tern still return to their rookery
on *Motu Nui* where brave ghosts
swim back with eggs held high.

Female children, their legs spread wide,
still pose for the priests
who imprint their sex on stone.
Komari—the vulva glyphs—still
send their *mana* across a land
where men rule
and women birth children year by year.

XIII

The massive statues dead, this new ritual
gained in fervor, proclaiming
Tangata Manu winner from a winning clan
who lived in well-served isolation
until another spring unfolded and another youth
retrieved a new brown-spotted egg,
gaining prestige for the following year.

Revelers, dancers and chanters supported
the warriors and their servants.
The warriors gained or lost but their servants
like the carvers before them
braved the shark-infested waters,
sheltered in island caves,
swam back, the winning egg in hand.

Finally the Birdman cult also bowed
to depletion of time
and all the old ways faded
beneath the weight of unrecorded history.
If the Chilean supply ship fails to dock
flour is scarce. When planes land
the islanders gather to see who's come.

Birdman house at Orongo

Bermed roofs of Birdman houses at Orongo

XIV

Was it village or class war finally put an end
to Rapa Nui's golden years,
hunger, despair, external rage
or intimate despair?
The statues cast face down
no longer confront descendants,
mana streaming from their eroding eyes.

The great figures, splayed at the foot
of their crumbling *ahu*
relax in volcanic soil,
earth fills sockets
where eyes once shot their power
straight to waiting hearts.
Wind cries.

The sea stretches to a circular horizon
from Rapa Nui's pink sand coves
and craggy cliffs
undoing themselves to foam.
Sea of a blue that has no name,
a dozen blues, no name for any.
Beyond cobalt. Beyond turquoise.

Gift for a new era, when the essence
of giving shifts.
No longer will we draw
heat and breath
from lovers or progeny,
but fill ourselves with the time of the *moai*
walking home.

XV

Today, dogs that belong to everyone
and no one, sleek-coated dogs
roam the streets of *Hanga Roa*.
Rider-less horses gallop dusty sidewalks,
wait at unmarked crossings,
and look both ways before moving on.
Cattle graze among the fallen moai.

The tiny airport at *Hanga Roa* boasts
long Pacific runway:
alternative touch down
for the U.S. space shuttle if weather denies it
Cape Canaveral or California's coast.
Commercial flights to Tahiti and Chile
negotiate each new day.

As our plane descends, nosing toward tarmac
on your tiny triangle of land,
or lifts into the Pacific sky
headed for places in touch with other places,
a thick veil of time closes behind me,
eyes and ears shift and I breathe again:
that familiar register.

XVI

Now my dreams become places or a place
where time slips between grasses
choking the doors to secret harbors
of image, language, memory.
Barriers dissolve. A great shudder
invites me in, then throws
my body against itself.

What I saw, heard, felt, imprints itself
on the underside of skin.
What I left behind stays with me
in unexpected gravure.
By some arbitrary trick
I gained then lost four hours
for Rapa Nui's clocks strike Albuquerque time.

Rapa Nui's silent *moai* reach
from mysterious birth and death
across the waters of a cold Pacific
to where I wait
un-resigned to fading memory,
awkward, trembling, moved
to permanent response.

Moai inside Rano Raraku crater

Moai on outer flank of Rano Raraku

Pulling the
Island Behind

Poetry is not a stage, but a constituent of human consciousness.

– Anne Waldman*

* Anne Waldman, *Outrider*, Albuquerque, La Alameda Press, 2006.

Falling Moai on outer flank of Rano Raraku

Left Handed

I

As I watch you, stone-carver ghosts, chipping away
at your mammoth blocks of basalt or tuff,
coaxing prominent noses, pursed lips,
etching decorated ears
and smoothing hollows
where eyes will store and shoot their mana
to a hungry populace,

as I watch you chisel the line of an arm, dropped
to the side, bent slightly forward
to faint shadow of loincloth
fingers reaching for mirrored fingers,
when I observe you,
hammers and polishing-stones in hand,
kneeling in the narrow troughs

where rock still clings to rock and the giant figure
has yet to free itself,
begin its journey out of the quarry
down rocky slope to the platform
waiting by a vulnerable shore,
the ahu that will be its home,
its back to ferocious sea,

when I dream your rhythms, the focus in your eyes,
weeks or months to a single statue's birth
—long sheets of rain,
heightening the echo of your song,
hundreds working together

or ten or twelve—
I always wonder

if your left hand, like another's left foot
in a distant land
and years into future, or the words
that spill too soon from a troubled mouth
knew what had to be done
and how. Were you left-handed
is my question, one of many.

II

Right hemisphere walks out
across a field of volcanic rock
spewed and settled
before the rising of time.

Bare feet resist daggers
of hardened obsidian,
blood tangles with dry earth
as rhythm dulls pain.

Which side of the brain
designs your palm frond hat,
places a flower
behind your listening ear?

Pulling the Island Behind

1

The most isolated inhabited spot on earth,
as distant from Iraq or Afghanistan
—or the United States—
as any place can be,
also suffers from colonialism
(Chilean variety)
as it lurches toward modernity.

LAN and Air Tahiti Nui flights
bring travelers, cargo, mail.
There are Internet cafes
on *Hanga Roa's* main street,
and while letters are still retrieved
from a single post office
and no traffic lights blink red and green,

the island cemetery is looking to expand
its hallowed ground
and seasons are stretched taut
between elders who guard
the traditional ways
and entrepreneurs—local
and foreign—

who lust to move forward, pulling
their island behind.
Culture, language, memory: all hang
in delicate balance between menace of future
and ancient loneliness,

crowded by long grass,
crumbling *ahu,* sinking *moai.*

II

In a Baghdad market the woman's clouded vision
revives in this child at her breast
who watches two hundred pair of straining legs,
two hundred shoulders push
against the great stone figure
while holding it back
lest it fall and shatter.

Imperceptible to woman or child
this instant of surprise
replacing everything known
with everything known.
Old language
supersedes the new:
brief glyph of sound.

III

If only we could learn to trust
non-linear time
to fix our wrongs,
coax a gentle hand
from onslaught of war
and greed, inhabit
another chance at getting it right.

If we could spin seven billion lives
in one kaleidoscopic pulse
of glass chips
morphing from deep red
to early morning pallor,
until the last spilled blood
and tears dry,

causing the most isolated spot on earth
and the most ravaged
to birth a future that signals future.

Migration

I

Migration haunts these times
as millions flee defeat
lured on by safety, food or water,
cross borders stitched shut
at rivers, fences, walls
or decisions made in distant rooms
by men with bullets in their mouths.

Border desert, pockmarked by bodies
of those who paid the *coyote*
then succumbed to thirst
and sun, their dreams
vacating dying eyes,
unable to reach exploitation:
too hot, too tired, too lost.

Land mines rip limbs from children,
their mothers carrying
the same will to keep them safe
as you, as I. Geographies
break apart on the empty eyes
or cracked lips
of lives whittled to fading survival.

II

Ancient migration routes traced currents,
rises and hollows in the earth's
poor crust, stars or roads
straight as the meridian
from Chaco north to Aztec
and south to Paquimé
where feathers and pots and shells

abandon and retrieve a fragmented story
pieced together
by archaeologists and satellites
scientists and poets,
each savoring the clues
that braid the story
crouched in a single bottomless heart.

III

Trade routes. A condor flying low
over densely-painted green.
The cleft in rock
where water was traded
for perfume, spices and metals.
Escape from another's war
or long time home.

Between the canyons of the Colorado
and Mayan kingdoms to the south,
geometric designs evolved
and settlements stand
like a trail of spent beads.

Questions climb
centuries of dust.

Between Mangareva and Easter
the routes defy hot winds,
changing currents and undertows.
Between Easter and Peru
slavery and disease
fly backward, defining exodus,
surprising rebirth.

IV

The routes are not lines but spirals
sinking and climbing,
breathless and slowing,
searching only for a land
where quiet replaces
the hard-wired questions
of an agitated heart.

Ahu Tehai

Makemake petroglyph at Orongo

Ahu Akapu

Inhabitants

Again and again they return:
loop of migration
to the old places.
Lifetimes, generations,
where grinding stone
worked childhood corn,
ceramic pots offered polished lips,
a granary known only to the elders
looked down upon
the log thrown across entrance
in or out.

Each return tethers the anchor,
rebuilds time on beloved land,
closes or opens a door.

Accidental. Misplaced.

– Elinor Davidson Randall, my mother
January 20, 1910 – November 17, 2006

Days before she will die she raises
a muscled arm, grabs
the sharp knobs
of surf-drenched lava.
Crab-like, her splayed fingers sure,
bare feet pushing off and up,
she climbs the treacherous cliff.

Ninety-six and never athletic,
this is her dream:
gnarled and slippery
from the comfort
of narrow nursing-home bed.
Nursing home dream
as window or calling card.

It can't be long now. She is sure:
twentieth-century woman
whose years spill awkward
across the century's divide.
Long pauses,
desert where memories disappear
behind a rose-colored butte.

Instant information, digital drama,
confusing telephone menus
and sorry patronage.

She is tired
and ready to move on
to whatever confident promise
or nothing at all.

We do not recognize the feedback loop
this shore or that
as we make the transition:
this body to another, this time
to past or future time,
different millennia or location
unsuspected and unclear.

Now she no longer remembers the dream.
Accidental. Misplaced.

Matriarch Now

– on my mother's death

Your raptor heart approaches,
backs away, chides or knocks
my awkward memory and time,
dares to cradle as it topples me again.

Its ragged beat returns me
to hospice monitors, their fluorescent lines
spiking and settling, speaking
a language I struggled to decipher

those last days, your institutional room,
the dying implacable, the march
ongoing, purposeful
as your tiny body lay in morphine peace:

quiet except for your breathing,
shallow gulps rasping air
but no discomfort you insisted, no pain.
Again you asked "are they happy?"

about your son's relationship, the same
about interchangeable grandson and his wife.
"Oh, that's good," you smiled again,
reassured we're alright,

nothing more for you to do.
A generosity of spirit I'd rarely seen
lit those last four days as you
embraced and joked and spoke

of "the miracle of good care. This is
so wonderful" you repeated
to our astonishment, "I am
so happy."

At 96, finally choosing the time,
deciding to let go,
loving the visits
then asking they stop,

wanting only a pain-free end
with us beside you. There was music:
a 'cello and Indian flutes. No flowers.
Words that meant what they said

until there were no more words
from you—only from us, your children
saying what we
could not say before.

Your eyes lost to us then, fixed
somewhere beyond our horizon.
Death: wrenchingly difficult
or peaceful as sleep. Either way

its echo knifes me
these hours before full clarity of dawn
beckons me forward:
uncertain matriarch now.

Remembered Lives

We are shocked and repelled, hold ourselves
above such tales
of conquerors and captives,
hearts and livers
cut from terrified bodies
or bodies soothed in peyote trance,
stone altars dripping blood.

Great museums display the altars,
artistic monuments
we circle in their majesty
freed by separation and time,
unwilling to scratch
the scrubbed patina
of our shadowy belief.

We do not want to hear the stories
of death in the trenches,
Hanau Eepe ambushing *Hanau Momoko,*
Long Ears against Short, one clan
pushing another
into a place of no escape,
caves where people ate their own.

Cannibalism among the Ancestral Puebloans
too, heritage of skulls
boiled in ancient pots,
savaged bones, feces deposit
whitened by age and air
bearing telltale DNA
impossible to ignore.

Barbarians, we say, uncivilized cultures
whose criminal ways
we claim not to understand,
cannot accept
and must not repeat.
Grasping at justification, mumbling
words designed as cover-up.

Yet within our time there is
Auschwitz and Bergen Belsen,
fangs surgically-implanted
into rebel jaws, children
taken in torture, given to families
where torturers rule, a fatwa
threatening the writer.

A killing field where human skulls
remain, mute testimony
to betrayal.
While elsewhere on the globe
Hutus still wield their machetes
against Tutsis
in Rwanda's sickened memory.

Women buried alive with the corpses
of their husbands, girl children
cut and sewn against the crime of desire,
nations destroyed by other nations
with the power to destroy.
Professed ignorance now all it takes
to survive immune.

No nation, no century, no island lost
in the vastness of hope
escapes what we have done
and continue to do to one another
in the name of necessity,
in the name of greed, progress
or some newer version of the lie.

How to Believe

We have sixty or seventy years
ninety if from sturdy stock
half that or less
if ours is hunger's history
war
all the unnatural deaths.

My childhood kept age irrelevant
mirrors returned
odd pieces
of where I would go
then vines grew
in expansion of flesh.

Even then I did not inhabit that flesh
until one morning dark canyons
and the high water mark
on a granite wall
leapt through reflection
into my eyes.

Lived years nestle in my shoulders now.
Who knows what
quickens my pulse
or waits for me.
I am left with a single question:
how to believe?

Storyline

I

Chaos below the Third Avenue El
fixes a harness across her breast.
Mother can't risk her breaking loose,
sudden screech of traffic or some strange hand,
doesn't know grandfather already enters
her invisible rooms.
Later she tears the straps,
defines direction as anywhere bad girls go.

She comes by stubbornness honestly,
remembers all her mother needed to hear
was: Don't visit Bolivia
there's been a revolution,
and family-strong
they cross the *altiplano* on a winter train,
descending to *La Paz,*
one corpse still swinging from a metal post.

Surely she imagines that corpse
woven deftly into her storyline,
images serving her writer's eye
as scenes multiply:
sleeping naked on sun-baked desert rock,
exploring ghost towns,
and the tongues of boys
no older and much less brave than she.

II

Time to move stage left, she travels
to a distant city
where artists work in cold-water lofts
meaning lifts itself in paint
and early poems
breathe pussy-willow shy.
She listens, lays down, stands up
and gives birth to a son
who forever after makes her two.

Her storyline curves outward, left again
and south to a different sound
whose syllables refuse
to come in from the rain
and inhabit her poems
but teach her to know and love
in another voice, stand with
those bludgeoned by the monster
she sees each time she opens her eyes.

Tlaloc lashed to an eighteen-wheeler
circles the place
Quetzalcoatl plays with serpent and *nopal,*
water pours from blue sky.
The poet who's lost his voice
tells her this and she is there,
living the scene he utters:
poor tongue longing for easier speech.

Pentimento walls catch white doves
in flight,
target splashes of red paint,

a *plaza* where hundreds die,
milk pail at dawn and death
falling either side of an ominous fence.
Later that fence moves north
splits a nation: language
unfit for any poem.

||||

Then an island draws her to righteousness,
storylines compete
and children *nacen para ser felices,*
born to be happy in the words of revolution.
Map cut from the fabric of world,
energy flowing in every direction
sugar today
oil tomorrow,
fairness speaking her name.

She stuffs her script deep in pockets then
and deep in her children's pockets,
for now she is five
or six if she counts the man
but the man keeps changing,
ripping patches of her skin
as he disappears.
He cannot erase the woman
for she fashions a safe house,
only sometimes misplacing the key.

Sometimes she works so hard
to remember where she hides that key,
where flesh clings to spit and bone
and a small boat docks.

She and her children climb aboard
row with or against the current.
They follow her
until they don't anymore,
auditioning on their own.

IV

Her story merges with
all the others then,
clamors like those in the poem
where one comes and begs the corpse:
Please don't die, get up and move,
and two come and ten and
a hundred thousand beseech the corpse,
and the dead man slowly rises to his feet
to inhabit another body,
battle or time.

Her storyline splits apart. She crosses borders
but pieces get left behind,
sprout small fingers and toes,
kick clods of earth,
find comfort in loneliness.
Men design master plans
and women make theirs
but the men swallow
the women's plans:
all in a good day's work.

She knows that un-chewed food
is wrong, sickens and pollutes.
Others begin to notice.
Courage replaces patience

on the list of good-girl traits,
and storylines come together
like magnets
connecting and growing
into a play with many characters,
all stitching promise to need.

We practice long and hard
from the turkey feathers
tied in ancient alcoves,
grain we mill
with our own hands
horizons calling us
through long canyons
into sunlit valleys
where we discover
a growing season.

V

Her storyline lingers among
nacatamales and dream,
tears that stopped flowing
come now in a cellular rush.
Trust clings to skin
stretched much too tight
and she gathers herself
as the B-movie man
becomes Commander in Chief,
promising an end to history.

She hauls her story north once more
to the place her umbilical cord
would welcome her

had her family kept tradition.
Even assimilated Jews depend on ritual
when weather mourns:
a lifeline for the lean times
come to a screeching halt
when all seems lost.

Strands of her story flung like loops
of rope: fishing nets on a Naxos pier
little red floaters
dotting the egg-yoke fiber
kept safe from Aegean blue.
One strand decides to fight
breathes hard against official dictum
declares herself home,
intends to stay.

Another reinvents love, retrieves trust
from a pile of worn garments
laid out by the fire
its flames rage high,
threaten to engulf her
if she chooses convention,
crooked speech closing her throat.

One strand whispers it's time to remember
time to focus
on the story without a name,
the one he told her never to tell
even when she was too young
too tender for words,
intuition alone
running interference in her veins.

VI

Strands merge. Love comes.
Battles are won in quiet
as in pain.
Her story settles into place
where horror claims
the right to murder and hate.
Unspeakable acts
committed in her name.
But she says no.

All she can do is say no.
It is never enough.
While her storyline etches itself
in solid rock
her children weave their lives
and their children too,
and she loves the woman beside her
who loves her back.
Years hold them all.

Her storyline merges with those still walking
through jungles or to the edges of cliffs
follow ancient roads
carry babies up *moqui* steps
carved into vertical space.
She runs her tongue over teeth
ground low by sandstone in the corn
and wonders what language
will open her mouth.

She wants to believe every age
imposes death upon peoples
grabs more than its share
turns its back on water and on sun.
She wants to believe
we will survive, revive,
her great grandchildren free
to claim their places on another stage.

Feet Still Run

– Tlatelolco, October 2, 1968

I

Se les pasó la mano I heard someone say,
they went too far: irony as release
as if anyone believed
they'd fired to disperse the crowd.

It was early. We didn't know
the number of victims,
didn't know we would never know
who died that day.

White arm bands moving through the crowd,
bullets shattering air
over Aztec stone, between colonial walls
and modern apartment blocks.

Feet still run in every direction
leaving shoes, a beret, a handbag
trampled in the *Plaza de las tres culturas*
as the trapped still fight their way

into buildings, pound on doors, plead
with terrified neighbors
locked down against sudden war,
cutting lights, swallowing fear,

retreating to silence, pretending
the stairwells aren't sticky with blood
bodies aren't piled on bodies
two stories high.

‖

What power does when threatened
is what we learned
that afternoon
thirty-nine years ago,

and displacement: rekindled images
of World War Two refugees
ghosts in slow lines
carrying households on their heads.

Parents making the rounds
of hospitals and morgues
staring into each bloated face
for signs of a son, a daughter.

Your knock at my door, your
random rush of words:
how you managed to take refuge
in one of the apartments

got out the next morning
hugging the arm
of the woman of the house
going for breakfast milk.

The 1968 Olympic Games
took place as promised.
White doves stenciled over graffiti
bleached the city for visiting crowds.

We entered night streets then
threw small bags of red paint

at each dove's breast.
And still, the city was mute.

]]]

Against the silence, whispers
of three hundred or a thousand dead,
students lined up behind the church
shot without charge or trial.

The Games went on, the athletes
only concerned
with winning their sport,
doing their country proud.
When two from the United States
raised their black-gloved fists
they where protesting
apartheid in South Africa

but we could pretend
they saw Mexico
stood with us
in our pain.

All these years later whispers, names,
numbers still crouch in alleys
wail across the *pedregal*
up the steep sides of mountain shantytowns

safely hidden
from a cosmopolitan city center
relentlessly competing its way
into the twenty-first century.

IV

Every October second I wake remembering
what I cannot forget
have never forgotten
but store with all those other memories

pushed down where their sad mix
raises bile.
What power is capable of
when threatened

or in the words
of the *Tarahumara* man
who ran a thousand kilometers south
to lend his community's support:

"We've always known what they've done to us
but when they murder
their own sons and daughters
we know they are evil."

Neither our most devastating war
nor closest in time,
just me learning
how far they are willing to go.

How far they will go.

Surprising Burma

If I walk into that canyon ahead of the rain
I may never finish this poem
about the unsettled feeling
all those news reports surprising Burma
shove against my vocal chords.
Air moves uncertainly
and yes, I say Burma

though who's to say a name
carved by colonial power
trumps one writ by a home grown junta
uniformed and stony faced
photographed handing packages of foreign aid
to those who were not carried mercifully
upon such floodtide of death?

If I walk into that canyon or die
before rearranging these words one final time,
if I let another event distract the doubt
shadowing news flashes yet again,
I may lose Aung San Su Kyi's determined face
or turn my back on the monk who wants us to know
the birds stopped singing after the storm.

I must scour the gap between revelation and truth,
pieces of a puzzle that do not fit,
edges that fail to come together.
The facts are these. A powerful cyclone
ripped across the Irrawaddy Delta
leveling holograms of resignation
in its path.

In that invisible nation of monks and peasants
quiet perseverance, quiet thunder,
they say four thousand, then
twenty-two thousand, a hundred thousand
and more than a million survivors wait
while we hold in our hands
what pretends to be news.

But something is wrong. Sound bites
direct the traffic of our minds
inflection coerces trust.
Disaster always tugs at a heart in safety,
who doesn't want to help?
We are told U.S. naval vessels just happened to be off shore
just happen to have relief supplies at the ready

but the generals will not let them in.
And we hate those generals
because we know what they did to brave protestors
only months before,
how their weapon is isolation
meant to silence brutality, torture, death:
all those practices we attribute to others.

The truth but not the whole truth
rises in empty spaces peopled with broken lives
while death comes up half noun half verb
throws mud in eyes that try to believe what they see
what the experts tell us about people
a century distant
who only want to be free.

Because the generals accept the gift but not the giver
some aid is stopped.

India is welcome, China too,
but here United States equals world.
Again we are shown
a man stitching his house together,
a woman huddled on a platform of sticks.

We cannot trust those generals to deliver
anything but loss
yet loss shames memory,
the Hail Mary play
borne on a wave of rotting food, disease, despair.
Loss of a name, a word
meaning one thing today another tomorrow.

The world cannot trust the generals
to distribute the aid on their own.
Yet we trust ourselves:
we who gave to Europe's Jews, the living ghosts
of Latin America, New Orleans in water's wake,
ask nothing in return.
Will generosity come up noun or verb today?

Something waits its turn
along this puzzle's crumbling edge,
something waits for someone to say:
Look, I was there all along
but you didn't recognize my face.
If I walk into that canyon
or die before finishing this poem

will a storm called Nargis, Burma or Myanmar,
refuge of monasteries, evil of generals
fade beneath the weight
of the world's next natural disaster

while sound bites aim their arrows
and photos promising not to lie
block our information highway

with another story of another people
somewhere else
we are persuaded to imagine
robbed of history, stopped in time?

Calamity or Stagecraft

We do not experience ourselves as part of nature
but as an outside force destined to dominate and
conquer it. We speak of battling nature, forgetting
that if we win the battle we will still be on the
losing side.

– E.F. Schumacher[*]

1

We speak, sing, bequeath our words
to future travelers
who visit the old places
searching for our stories
as we search for the stories
of those who left their clues
on high ledges of winter stone.

Questions leak out. Did the people move
north to south or south to north,
are these horny toads—one etched in black
the other always painted red—
sign of a single culture or two,
each accessing the ritual symbol
from a different direction?

Creative beings, we assume
art textured this utilitarian bowl,
etched design upon the handle
of this tool.

[*] E. F. Schumacher, *Small is Beautiful, Economics as if People Mattered*,
Hartley and Marks, 1999, p. 4.

We find it easy to believe
earlier humans chose or created
what was beautiful
as they bartered food, warmth, safety.

II

Is desire always beautiful,
generosity, shadow,
numbers, cycles and circles,
ease or comfort, a footprint
in the muddied riverbed?

Are caution and risk
things of beauty,
each in its own time
to be spent when eyes close
and trees dance to the rhythms
of angry winds.

Is the snow crystal visible
only to the practiced eye?

III

The supernova that lit the sky
in AD 1054
was visible midday
bright as a full moon
bathing the night sky
in ruby light.

The volcano that turned
this desert inside out
buried eight hundred
square miles of land
in glowing cinders,
spewing liquid rock
for miles.

Then Halley's comet appeared
trailing its white tail
way up there,
sign and signifier.
And a rash of black spots
not seen before or since
blemished a stalwart sun.

Unfolding sequence traveling
through a single generation.
An offering. A nest.
While you flashed
pyrite or obsidian mirrors
from rise to rise.

Armature of calamity
or stagecraft of the highest order?

Corn

In ancient America, amaranth
meat and beans
released the niacin in corn,
rendering it safe to eat.

Stalks supported gold, rust, blue-black,
stones ground kernels to fine powder,
green leaves enfolding our mother
danced with us through the night.

Corn eaten in abundance and alone
depletes serotonin in the brain
brings sleep deprivation, aggression,
a dangerous ecstasy.

Chaco, at the center of everything,
fashioned the same knives
used to cut out beating human hearts
a thousand miles to the south.

Cultural dementia: life's other face
wherever we are.

You Get to Choose Now

The question enters on fierce wind
baby cactus quills riding its breath,
rears beside me begging acknowledgment.

I laugh, dissimulate dis/ease
remember your careful fingers
picking those other quills from my sore breast.

At the equator
Ecuador
line as fragile as being forced to choose

I'd leaned in to photograph one waxy bloom
my camera lens erasing distance.
This question stands a generation older

brushing the same breast
claiming the same ribbed space
in time and memory.

Leap the interrogation mark—my aging body says—
nurture answers where they grow.
Choose where you turn your eyes.

Whole Silence

Inside this silence
new words pass
through the birth canal
wide angle springs
to long focus and back

dark spider matrix spreads
across perfect turquoise face.
Memory's after-image
crawls back
to comfort after the flood.

Rejected by fear
I hold out my hands
stroke this new presence
where a darker silence
mocks my undoing.

No longer seeking what's gone
I welcome what rises
to greet me in its place.

Always There Is a Place

Through struggle the abused can achieve
a kind of dignity that puts the abuser to shame.

– David Cole

How do I arrange myself
against the State
when poison arrows
still find their mark
between my eyes?

How not lose this voice
slower but soaked
in cherished blood?
My comrades:
reach back and take my hand.

Always there is a place
off limits to evil.
Always there is
a place of dignity
they cannot invade or occupy.

The Art of Our Love

Pondering days
you decide on an orange line
but leave the paper white
behind the ram's left leg.

Is it a ram? Only the man
who etched the figure to rock
eight hundred years ago
can say for sure.

Was it a man?
We do not know but I
know your androgynous hand
sizzles with ancient energy

as it retrieves
the wandering and the dream,
bringing them home
to this small square of paper.

Those who speak of art
call it negative space.
It takes my breath away

and I would have it
no other way, love,
nowhere but you
calling me back to your studio.

Come have a look
you say,
or me calling you
to read my newest poem.

Our house of art
propelling this tornado in my heart.

The A Word

Imprisoned skin, blanched of color, your face
turned to mine, teetering
between the question you could not speak
and that promise of honesty, so easy
to honor when all is well.

I held my breath, then could wait no longer.
Is it the lost words, empty spaces,
silences? Are you afraid,
I asked, afraid myself of your answer.
You admitted you were, and cried.

I held you then, my cheek to your fear,
slowly explained my movement
in and out of silence,
reminded you senility—the dreaded A word—
stumbles in one direction only.

Four years down the road I still remember
how I shifted my own dis/ease to comfort yours,
reassured and calmed your hostage eyes,
remember how we held one another,
our breathing slowing to a safer place.

All our time since that question—48 months,
1,460 days, weeks, hours, minutes
sure in one another's presence.
Oh yes I hold each perfect frame of time:
wildflowers bright beside the road.

Singular Shadow Rock

Earth's fingers, stark yet molten,
run to a valley still stretching
still expanding its chest
with gulps of brilliant desert air.

Ridges spill inked mineral
fading to bleached ravines
falling onto esplanades
where salt bubbles a rutted surface.

My breath follows earth's contour
shapes singular shadow rock:
afterimage of desire. Where I go
Death Valley tags my heels,

sets me ablaze.

Disappearing Beauty

Soft rain cools canyon air
turns streaks of desert varnish
rich dark brown,
the boulders where I place my hands
a brilliant red.

Delicate columbine blooms
from a crack where earth
cannot be found,
scant as my breath
as I struggle up the fault.

Searching the next mile post
and the next, no trail
but faint footsteps of those
who preceded us here
rising to meet the searching eye.

What magnet pulls me
to where these people
—ancestors only in desire—
moved through disappearing life,
mouthing invented syllables?

Perhaps nothing more or less
than my need
to raise disappearing beauty
where wars of greed
pile against exhausted memory.

A Word Breaks

A word breaks
along its fault line.
Blue crystals
rise behind my eyes.

Sentences wander
in four directions,
promise to regroup
when sun goes home.

A dust storm folds me
into its spinning arms.
I rise, I float
and never say I'm sorry.

Relativity

– for Martín

My grandson breathes
time's relativity,
slow passage
in a boring class,
flight when he sleeps
or is engaged.
He imagines
an invisible roller coaster
more exciting for its riders.

This edge of life
time's structure moves erratic
insists on
multi-dimensional curve of space
sucked into the black hole
or spun elliptical around its mouth
and flung beyond our universe,
perfectly describing
the time I know.

Left hand's brief tremble
reaches for my grandson's prism,
savors its possibilities
as I wonder how much longer
I will hold the camera
or—quite a different question—
how soon I won't.
Relativity being relative
where I walk.

Single sentence stretches
hoping to grab
the necessary word
or even some look-alike
breaking the silence
that invades this room.
Between amusement
and rage
I choose defiance.

In Quick Succession

All my days arrive and leave
in quick succession.
One ends, another begins
demarcation barely raising its head
above the fray.

The fray is on automatic now,
no way of stopping
this machinery of age,
all that memory
locked into focus.

Yesterday revived
is tomorrow waiting its turn in line
while 24 frames per second
speed to a color
never before imagined.

And when I must wait for a word
—a question's lost answer
or answer's hidden question—
there is patience
for what I know will return

and that time too moves effortlessly
on silent rollers.
Even my heartbeat slows to accommodate
equal measure of what has gone
and what is yet to come.

Perfect balance between the two
hurtles me into a future
already cradled
in my arms:
a past regained.

Between the Old Year and New

– for Linda Gilkey and Nancy Parker Wood,
murdered in their car, New Year's Eve 2006.

Sometime between the old year and new
horror leaps to your eyes
and life stops
with a sound too loud, too harsh.

Did he watch you kiss? Was there a kiss
or look, some sign of unacceptable love
that triggered his rage?
Perhaps he knocked on your car window,

perhaps you lowered it to ask
if he needed help. Snow fills the air
as he shoots you in the face, then fires
a second time at your lover's chest,

the woman your obituary called good friend,
who shared your life
where dogs and cats
still wait for you to come home.

Moon Colony

To colonize the moon, something
like a huddle of trailers
the reporter's voice explains

providing space primacy,
a base
from which further explanation

may spring. A sour churning
rises in my belly,
coats throat and tongue,

denies my voice full range.
A trailer park
on that body of mystery

mimicking what our ancestors
did to the Indians
our parents tried in Vietnam

we attempt today in Iraq.
Except now
we know how it turns out,

what happens when men invade and claim,
what is comfortably lost,
stop it from growing.

More Sugar?

As long as there's blood
as long as violence
fills the mind's eye, eye's eye
as long as there's fear
shock and awe from a ready field
of those who look different act different
speak a different language
whose rituals
we do not recognize.

As long as breath stumbles
and falls
heart climbs into the throat
its beat overpowering sense
and sensibility,
threatening eardrums,
memory, the resource
of a steady hand.

As long as memory bends and breaks
beneath low whisper of terror.
As long as power stands ordained
in a war we cannot smell or feel
its temperature swallowing
someone else's home

where car or bridge
or human body
tears shatters comes apart
and someone has snapped the shutter

so we may repeat our witness:
Greek chorus
to the groomed psyche.

As long as this season's reality show
mimics without regret,
the dead speak,
fear grabs, rivets, pulls us
beyond our safety zone.

As long as the picture of the year
Oscar Emmy Golden Globe
winning song lyric, new release
and presidential discourse
remain interchangeable,
the senator asks, the general answers
and Channel 7 tells us it is so.

Or maybe they are CEOs
standing together
raising right hands
swearing they didn't know
only following orders, war is hell.
Gave 'em plenty of warning,
Couldn't tell they were children.
Just a few bad apples.

As long as boys will be boys
she's a slut he's a pussy
God's will be done
the Bible tells us chain of command
doesn't end until the last coon is dead
last slant-eye, kike, spic, faggot,

pervert, commie, a-rab, diaper head,
go back where you came from
America for Americans I say.

As long as the camera zeroes in
on another decomposing body
blood oozes across the screen
tips our balance
and the requisite number of seconds
provokes the desired jolt,
no more.
I was blinded by the color red.

Horror is measured
in ever-expanding increments
and we settle back
savor our forkful of microwave dinner
and reach for a sip of lemonade.
More sugar, anyone?

Seven Words

Seven words forbidden on radio or TV
while innuendo abuses a name
what the latest remedy can do for you
and swift-boat becomes a verb
that changes history.
These taunts pass the censors,
embedding themselves in memory.

Embed itself a word or concept
we are asked to accept,
questioning neither allegiance
nor source.
Reporting what men do
an idea whose time has come
and gone.

Flag-covered coffins
erased from the nightly news
but vacant eyes and severed limbs
make acceptable fare
as long as the dead don't look like us
and we believe the murder of an eight-year-old
was self-defense.

The seven words do not include
ho or heathen,
terrorist applied to a child
wandering into the conqueror's line of fire.
Beep beep beep beep
beep beep beep
always gets a laugh

while sovereign state morphs to evil empire
and the line between invade and occupy
stumbles and dies.
Liberate may be spoken
but shouldn't
and hope, change and peace
are reborn as holograms.

Lie. Lie if you must, if you can
and repeat the lie
until it closes the window
on what we know.
Denial will take up the slack
when evidence to the contrary
kicks us upside the head.

Imagine a Body

I say it is fear. Long way down
from this rocky ledge,
imagine a body
hurtling through air
its years shrinking to seconds
view of the world cut clean,
never, or never again.

I say it is hunger gnawing
at bellies and bones
simple arithmetic
between the teeth
who decides
who deserves to eat
and who to die.

I say what happens to them
can happen to us, you, me,
change of direction
no severance pay
or clean sheets
water salving
lips peeled horizon-dry.

I say denial, self-satisfied
suits, dash of color
the expensive tie.
I say greed
speaking to greed
pointing recognition's finger,
thank you and good day.

In an almost perfect world
they would have to answer
for their crimes.
In the world we have
we are grateful
for comforting discourse
hiding more of the same.

Midday Recognition

Two hundred foot long wall
its shallow alcove holds millennia of weather.
Those who ground red hematite
applied the creams and pale greens
sharpened charcoal stubs
ten thousand years ago.

Came from nowhere
going nowhere
as their cousins to the south
tell us
their single staircase symbol
etched in Ollyantaytambo stone.

Here in this desert river bed
—Horseshoe Canyon, Great Gallery,
state of Utah, American Southwest:
names layered upon reconstructed memory,
one foot after another,
call us through sand to silence.

Until we stand before these massive figures
swaying in heat's clouded mirror:
midday recognition
larger than life
triangular masks
balanced on tapering bodies.

Smaller humans face off against the rock
and startling mouth

or vulva
spews its trail of endless count.
Assembly, genealogy
all of us.

Today's interpreters speak of Holy Ghost
cannot move beyond themselves
cannot pierce this membrane of time
swirling about our ankles
picking our teeth
catching our breath in its tangled net.

Connective Tissue

Clean shaven white male face we are meant to trust
to believe the words
he reads from a prompter hidden off-screen
pulling his focus just right of our eyes

he reports the latest catastrophe shows us deadened eyes
swollen bellies and flies
always the flies
few victims take the camera face-on and we wonder

if his questions pierce the membrane that keeps
our sterile glance from their lives
or what remains of them.
The perfect lips continue to move

through our evening meal guided by prompter
script and advertising goals
the bottom line
always this season's balancing act

keeping us caring but not too much, consuming
as much as possible
believing we are informed
ready to move onto the next flood or fire

the next war produced as reality show, who
remains on the island, who has lost
more weight, won more money,
gets to keep the rose.

One raging conflict replaces another, invades the screen
pokes at consciousness
then fades
so we can ask our doctor if Lipotur or Lunesta

Zantac or Boniva is right for us, so we can
become the lithe young woman
beguiling our living room
note possible upper respiratory infection

fatigue or other symptoms as these may be signs
of a rare but serious side effect
sometimes fatal
profit trumping personal pain.

Watch for these side effects and call your doctor
before it's too late, no explanation
—who attacked first or why—
short circuits the brain

and we cannot ride to the end of the line, cannot
come to grips
with how things work, especially ourselves
the concern on his face, his lips

or maybe hers in this era of equal deception
we are meant to applaud
gender equality
the brilliantly orchestrated dumbing down

of those bewitched by the beautiful people
their moving parts
the overplay of music
luring us to the next frame

and the next, deconstruction swirling our features
dizzy
erasing connective tissue
breaking every bone.

Call and Response

I will hide the words inside my shadow,
its single dimension
will keep them safe, embrace
each sound and color,
pulling down
then growing again,
obedient only to light.

They may beat or rape me, tear me
from love, connection, breath.
My shadow will remain,
long as night's promise,
solid as place.
Nothing and no one
can take the words.

In a region of other syntax, unfamiliar
sound, they will wait
patient as morning,
sure as that expanse
of south Pacific ocean,
playful as the baby whale:
call and response.

In a future time, my words will return
in search of their echo,
community, memory,
tears spilling from closed eyes,
recognition
in every rise and hollow
on the map.

Necklace of Days

Light gathers itself in a great ball
now hanging close
in the darkness of space
now peeled to a delicate sliver
although its full body is visible
beneath the shroud that hides
a mottled skin.

Light dances silver on moving crests
of water, as waves break
against beach
and sun emerges to bring
another day to life.
Bursting from cloud
rays of light pierce a wet horizon.

Light gathers pale yellow, pink, orange
to dusk red
as sky moves before your eyes,
reflects in your gaze,
sometimes offering
a multicolored arc
bridging this island shore to shore.

When you close your eyes
it is gone,
returning again each time
you look:
a necklace of days
unfolding in every direction.
You are home.

What I Tell the Young When They Ask

Resist
fictitious argument
luring or barking at your door
Don't ask your doctor
if seduction is right for you
only his wallet knows for sure.

Resist
turning away
from that which gleams in the sun
covers itself with unfamiliar cloth
or pronounces words
you do not understand.

Resist
don't ask don't tell
because it requires a dance of deception
steps on your toes
grinds them into a bed
of broken glass.

Resist
smoke and fire
water coveted in plastic bottles
a planet
too warm for life
too bleak for skin.

Resist
de-sexed corn, ancient grain
forced beneath the knife

regeneration taken by force
a trail of paper bullets
murdering surely as those of steel.

Resist
those who make
better bullets and bombs
clusters of pain
designed to kill
when hunger takes too long.

Resist
uniform or priestly collar
disguised on a scale of one to ten
books and tablets telling you
what will save you
from yourself.

Resist
my country right or wrong
men promising sound bites
answering only what they want you to know
then riding their rigged smiles
into a house of purest white.

Resist
the one on top
pitting his god his catchy phrase
a tune that taunts your face
spits in your eye
erasing the life-giving stories.

Resist
losing the ones
who know your name

call you from sleep
filling your mouth with music
when you wake.

Resist
rules created for you alone
and all your sisters and brothers
born and unborn
for they threaten
morning's fragile light.

Resist
disappearing into little boxes
of perfect safety
where risk is nowhere
greed is the prize
success thickens in your veins.

Resist
erasure of all our histories
for the sake of your
one and only life.
Listen to the small sounds.
Open your eyes.

Ahu Tongariki, seen from the lip of Rano Raraku crater.

AhuTongariki

Acknowledgments

My poetry is always enriched at public readings. The faintest murmur of audience response can move a word or line in another direction. I have also been fortunate to be able to count on others' critical attention to my work. This book has benefited greatly from the suggestions of Mark Behr, Barbara Byers, and Susan Sherman. Shawn McLaughlin, eminent Easter Island scholar and author of its best guidebook, was exceptionally generous in his critique, always willing to answer a question or point me toward a relevant study or article. Jane Norling's life as an artist parallels mine as a writer; I feel we often speak the same language in different mediums. She accompanied Barbara and me in March of 2007 on the trip to Rapa Nui that gave birth to many of these poems, and I am deeply grateful for her exquisite cover art. Finally I would like to thank Bryce Milligan for his care and attention in the production of this book; I have never had the pleasure of working with a more astute or knowledgeable poetry editor.

About the Author

Margaret Randall is a feminist poet, writer, photographer and social activist. She is the author of over 80 books. Born in New York City in 1936, she has lived for extended periods in Albuquerque, New York, Seville, Mexico City, Havana, and Managua. Shorter stays in Peru and North Vietnam were also formative. In the 1960s she co-founded and co-edited *El Corno Emplumado / The Plumed Horn,* a bilingual literary journal which for eight years published some of the most dynamic and meaningful writing of an era. From 1984 through 1994 she taught at a number of U.S. universities.

Randall was privileged to live among New York's abstract expressionists in the 1950s and early '60s, participate in the Mexican student movement of 1968, share important years of the Cuban revolution (1969-1980), the first four years of Nicaragua's Sandinista project (1980-1984), and visit North Vietnam during the heroic last months of the U.S. American war in that country (1974). Her four children— Gregory, Sarah, Ximena and Ana—have given her ten grandchildren. She has lived with her life companion, the painter and teacher Barbara Byers, for the past two decades.

Upon her return to the United States from Nicaragua in 1984, Randall was ordered to be deported when the government invoked the 1952 McCarran-Walter Immigration and Nationality Act, judging opinions expressed in some of her books to be "against the good order and happiness of the United States." The Center for Constitutional Rights defended Randall, and many writers and others joined in an almost five-year battle for reinstatement of citizenship. She won her case in 1989.

In 1990 Randall was awarded the Lillian Hellman and Dashiell Hammett grant for writers victimized by political repression. In 2004 she was the first recipient of PEN New Mexico's Dorothy Doyle Lifetime Achievement Award for Writing and Human Rights Activism.

To Change the World: My Life in Cuba, was recently published by Rutgers University Press. "The Unapologetic Life of Margaret Randall" is an hour-long documentary by Minneapolis filmmakers Lu Lippold and Pam Colby. It is distributed by Cinema Guild in New York City.

For more information about the author, visit her website at www.margaretrandall.org.

About the Cover Artist

Bay Area artist Jane Norling makes artwork that promotes social justice. For forty years as painter, graphic designer, poster artist and muralist, she has combined the sensibilities of fine art with the tools of design to create imagery that strongly advocates a point of view.

In her ongoing series of abstract landscape paintings, "Shaped By Water," Jane expresses her profound love of the natural world in explorations of the visual relationship of water to land. Her compositions evoke specific places she has visited as well as expressing a broader interpretation of place. Engaging with the sculpted evidence of water's actions over time and of human impact on landscape, Jane considers the global redistribution of water, its equitable access and the need for careful management. Her environmental concerns are part of the creation of each piece, emotionally, if not in subject matter. In creating them, she hopes to evoke in viewers a connection to familiar experiences with the natural world and to encourage in others their own exploration.

Norling visited Rapa Nui with Margaret Randall and Barbara Byers on the trip that inspired this book. The cover painting was made from a photograph taken as they picnicked high on the inner rim of Rano Raraku crater.

Jane Norling lives in Berkeley, California with her husband Bob Lawson, a union activist. Her son Rio Chávez is a musician in Chicago. See more of Norling's art and contact her at www.janenorling.com.

Critical Praise for

Their Backs to the Sea

argaret Randall's *Their Backs to the Sea* is a major accomplishment from one of America's most radical poet-citizens. Randall travels here "beyond cobalt" and "beyond turquoise" to Rapa Nui to consider the implications of legend, lore, geography, geology, migration, conquest, slave economies, and the powerful, insistent and mysterious presence of the magnificent stone moai. whose backs are indeed to the sea. This stance—stoically away from—has far reaching implications for the investigative psyche, an inward twist toward a spiritual guardianship, perhaps. Who were they, those creators of the silent megaliths? Do empty sockets absent obsidian and coral "pull us into vacancy"? And who are we in our own craggy cliffs, in our own "disappearing pages of an ancient book"? Randall is here an "archeologist of morning" in the Olsonian sense, and invoked too is his stress on istorin, as the root of "history"—to find out for oneself. The book continues the braid of themes with further fierce inquiry from Baghdad to Chaco, north to Aztec and to powerful litanies of resistance. "Ridges are squeezed into giant fists" throughout. Randall's own photographs which thread the collection are powerful and stunning reclamations as well. Brava!"

– Anne Waldman
The Jack Kerouac School of Disembodied Poetics
Naropa University

heir Backs to the Sea shows me again why I have looked to Margaret Randall for a poetry & a life driven by many forces, multiple times & places, changing with a will to change that places her among the real & really forceful poets of our time. Beginning with an extended poem in many parts – an epic as "a poem including history"—she first covers the archaeology & ecology of a chosen subject, Easter Island (Rapa Nui in the language of its people), then swings outward in these & other poems, to explore an even larger world & her own history as one who moves inside it. The book as book is breathtaking, both her words & her photographic studies that together jump genres, to leave us with a kinetic, truly complex work of art.

– Jerome Rothenberg
author of *Traditions of the Sacred*

Where do history and poetry meet to produce a third space of interrogation, wonder, and resonance? They do here. *Their Backs to The Sea* is a cartography of ruin, of contested days, of reclamation and occupation, of origin myths, of homage to the mysteries of an Easter Island both real and imagined, of lives lived in the center of time, of bodies who speak because language is life. In these poems, language travels through intricate tunnels where histories concenter to harmonize: do not forget the blood stained plaza of Tlatelolco, do not forget Komari the vulva glyphs, do not forget non-linear time, do not forget Auschwitz, do not forget absence of shame, do not forget life's other face. Mystery, resistance, and grace haunt these pages. It is a pleasure, yes, even in the face of atrocity and loss, a pleasure to travel these pages because the reader can be sure that the path is not without beauty. Margaret Randall is a rare poet—a seasoned historian who has not forgotten the primacy of the imagination.

– Akilah Oliver, author of *The She Said Dialogues: Flesh Memory*

The ease with which one moves through this clean, clear music masks the depth at which it works to change us as we read, enlarging an inner life to make room for so much experience—an exploration of the rim of Rapa Nui, an aging mother's death, the uprising in Mexico during the '68 Olympics. Margaret Randall writes poems of sympathy, intelligence, and witness. Listen to the

small sounds, she tells us. Open your eyes. But the wonderfully ne-
gotiated distances between small sounds and clear sight generate the
poetic sense here of a working world, a poet functioning in a function-
ing universe, the full specificity of what the poem can do today.

– Samuel R. Delany, author of *Dark Reflections*

Wings Press was founded in 1975 by Joanie Whitebird and Joseph F. Lomax, both deceased, as "an informal association of artists and cultural mythologists dedicated to the preservation of the literature of the nation of Texas." Publisher, editor and designer since 1995, Bryce Milligan is honored to carry on and expand that mission to include the finest in American writing—meaning all of the Americas, without commercial considerations clouding the choice to publish or not to publish. Technically a "for profit" press, Wings receives only occasional underwriting from individuals and institutions who wish to support our vision. For this we are very grateful.

Wings Press attempts to produce multicultural books, chapbooks, CDs, DVDs and broadsides that, we hope, enlighten the human spirit and enliven the mind. Everyone ever associated with Wings has been or is a writer, and we know well that writing is a trans- formational art form capable of changing the world, primarily by allowing us to glimpse something of each other's souls. Good writing is innovative, insightful, and interesting. But most of all it is honest.

Likewise, Wings Press is committed to treating the planet itself as a partner. Thus the press uses as much recycled material as possible, from the paper on which the books are printed to the boxes in which they are shipped.

Associate editor Robert Bonazzi is also an old hand in the small press world. Bonazzi was the editor and publisher of Latitudes Press (1966-2000). Bonazzi and Milligan share a commitment to independent publishing and have collaborated on numerous projects over the past 25 years.

As Robert Dana wrote in *Against the Grain,* "Small press publishing is personal publishing. In essence, it's a matter of personal vision, personal taste and courage, and personal friendships." Welcome to our world.

Colophon

This first edition of *Their Backs to the Sea: Poems and Photographs*, by Margaret Randall, has been printed on 70 pound paper containing fifty percent recycled fiber. Titles have been set in Papyrus type, the text in Adobe Caslon type. All Wings Press books are designed and produced by Bryce Milligan.

On-line catalogue and ordering available at www.wingspress.com

Wings Press titles are distributed to the trade by the Independent Publishers Group www.ipgbook.com